FEMINISM AND RUIN
Rep-Destruction: Gossip, Innuendo, Accusation

A KAREN KELLOCK PICTURESTRIP

Written & Illustrated by

Karen Kellock Ph.D.

Manual for Superior Men

A complete theory based on Einstein physics,
Political Psychology, Systems Theory
and Archetypal Psychiatry.

FORMULA

All success attraction
All disease obstruction
All recovery elimination

You must fast on all three

OBSTRUCTIONS:

People
Habit
Food

FEMINISM AND RUIN

Get Jezebel outa your life or she'll ruin it with strife. Nothing's worse than a tyrannical harridan in the home with wimpy hubby acting like a silly pawn. Femal e bullying is most vicious, taking the form of reputation destruction, innuendo and gossip. Girls who bully have many friends, are socially skilled and act in groups: destroy reps/spread the scoop.

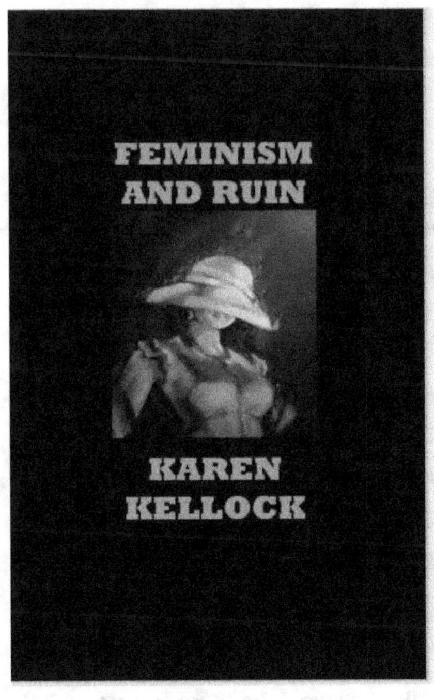

TRAPS OR YOUR MAP

What is the gist of a series on Social Psychology? That PEOPLE are the main obstruction honey.

People bothered me my whole life, it was enslavement. Then I got married and I was FREE man.

You're no one's option. Either you're number ONE or to hell with em, that's the way it is hon'.

How relieving to get into your own thing, far FAR away from the people's rantings, so frustrating.

Study a little, digest it a long while. Let it percolate all day in the sun and soon it's insight: wow!

No force-feed studying. I wanna let truths seep thru my system gradually, then real understanding.

Maybe Freud was right, it's all about sex. For soul ties are sexual and a universal/worldwide hex.

God told me to write these books because the problem is people-worship while the Almighty's forsook.

How an ego? The intelligentsia are the first to be killed off and dictators hate poets ya know.

PEOPLE ARE CRUEL/GETTING CRUELER

People are cruel and getting crueler. Get in your own bubble and stay there with your Savior.

Don't depend on people they won't be there tomorrow. Talk to your savior, tell HIm of your sorrow.

Study the holocaust, see what life can be like. When hate has the upper hand: mad max strife.

TRAPS OR YOUR MAP

Feel grateful for your circumstances as a gift from God. Never complain nor explain to the mob.

Gratitude is the key to God's heart. Make a list and think back to all the miracles from the start.

Teach kids how communism killed 100 million. They're taking us to hell, the brainwashed Millennials.

Yah the lessons were hard and painful, humiliating even. Get over it/go forward, palmy: triumphing.

Let those humiliations feed em: if they learn from your mistakes isn't that enough to teach em?

Let God take care of it this time, bring you two together. Just make a space & wait to be discovered.

There's no one like you on earth and everyone else will pale in comparison, that's God again.

I lived a life, much in the desert wilderness and now this, giving it all to you in a theory expressed.

WHY THEY DISCARD

Lovebombing is short-lived, it doesn't take him long to be disappointed in his love object.

Devaluation starts subtly. Veiled criticisms, failing to show, disinterest in talking, comparing.

She has a confusing, disorientating and painful sense of paradise lost from the flattery love blast.

The devaluation starts the empath on a downward spiral of confusion and despair: was he a liar?

After being seemingly loved and approved of she again feels crushed by her own defectiveness.

TRAPS OR YOUR MAP

She scrambles for answers: what've I done wrong? Her need to please & internal critic's hot now.

Failing: she makes frantic attempts to re-establish what they experienced during love bombing.

With unworthiness retriggered, it's harder than ever for the empath to reestablish as initial lover.

The narcissist feels rage as the other failed to meet the idealized partner they imagined them to be.

Even while devaluing the narc continues the union for supply, drip-feeding to reinforce the lie.

Narcissists use rewards/punishments hooking the other in despite the crushing disappointments.

From the high of being adored and loved to the low of being worthless and irredeemable.

The illusion of a perfect union is shattered in humiliating ways, as in him flaunting a new partner ok.

End shows a deep need to humiliate the other stripping her of all dignity while triggering jealousy.

A narcissist wants to destroy the other, hurting em is not enough. Recall that when in the dumps.

DOWNWARD SPIRAL WITH NARCISSIST

Empaths say they knew all along it was foolish flattery but the feel-good love chemicals were ecstasy.

Plus the attachment system was activated and that's all there was to it. And now she's lost all that?

Dopamine, serotonin: such chemicals made this a state of ecstasy and now she's down in hell see.

TRAPS OR YOUR MAP

She can't be grounded in her own authority with this going on. Knowledge is power, read on:

As all three systems are full throttle--attachment, need to please, inner critic--she falls of pedestal.

When she hits the wall her inner critic targets the narcissist rather than herself--and she's well.

She sought to please others while targeting herself, seeking only attachment--what a set up.

Teach your daughters how the empath interfaces with the narcissist and how they must resist it.

Teach about the holocaust: that'll make em humble for there is **NO** ego when tyranny's in control.

In a soul tie one is emotionally unavailable and the potential soul mate can tell/withdraws.

I JUST FOCUS ON MY FASTING

Ironic but true: the less you eat the healthier you'll be and fasting is the highest healer see.

Yes fruitarians lose all their hair but then it all grows back thicker/more lustrous/faster growth.

Hair loss as follicles are replaced is part of detox. The skin also gets worse then better, promise.

There are meat eaters, there are meat abstainers and there's no judgement either way for sure.

FEMINISM AND RUIN 1
Rep-Destruction: Gossip, Innuendo, Accusation

"I'm not angry I just have a hot temper and I'm passionate about certain things" she shrieked.

Women aren't born dumb they adapt to other women.

Female culture is a massive impediment to genius. Those who break through are rare variations.

Le Femme and the Communist Spirit: Wants open borders, approval of others, big government.

Nothing's more wrong than a liberal feminist and to think we had to adapt to that frustration as kids!

Races help each other up, so too religions and men do. But women push each other down, cruel.

What a sorry sight to see one so blind to their deficiencies and deep in denial: Hillary. Nigel Farage

Get Jezebel outa your life or she'll ruin it with strife.

It's been proven for decades in serious bully studies that female bulls are social/many friends.

FEMINISM AND RUIN 1

Nothing's worse than a tyrannical harridan in the home with wimpy hubby acting like a silly pawn.

Female bullying is most vicious, taking the form of reputation destruction, innuendo and gossip.

Girls who bully have many friends, are socially skilled and act in groups: destroy reps/spread the scoop.

Feminists: a genuine rape culture is spreading across Europe not a made-up one like yours.

Feminists complain about mansplaining or leg-spreading while Europe is conquered thru gang-raping.

The feminists hating males cuz they're a western man but then loving Jihadis, unbelievable.

The man-hating feminist wants to be crushed. She wants to be shoved around a little after all this.

"To keep em under control was not difficult--fill up their time/minds." Orwell

Consequence-free virtue signaling: a fundamentalist of feels.

Their virtue signaling is totalitarian: you dam well tow this line or we will call you unforgiving.

All you can do is stay away and if you do you'll be ok.

God gave me success when I learned to treat my husband right. Joyce Meyers

Have a fifties lifestyle no matter what's going on: lock the gate and concentrate on those at home.

What does it mean to be loved by a woman--does it mean to be broken so her vanity's not threatened?

Men are only mean when you act that way. In relationships be normal and decent and all is ok.

You can't trust women anymore guys--find one who didn't go to college.

Jezebel floozy: don't trust her just cuz the dogs and cats love her.

You thought she was stunning 'til you found out she was nothing and what a shock honey.

Education is destroying the soul. A Ph.D. with no common sense at all.

Having two liberal sisters/social mother I know all about women and like the plague avoid em.

Men are weak cuz their dads were gone, brought up by mom--its her anger when they speak.

Mom and two feminist sisters were illogical as Merkel and I often cried from the contradictions, hysterical.

You're not a misogynist cuz you're telling the truth about what women are doing.

If left approves cuz if you reinforce their weirdness they'll love you but you're going to hell miss.

If they want you nothing will keep em away but if they don't want you nothing will make em stay.

Patriarchy plus chivalry equals happy women and societies.

Sweeter they are the more virtue signaling but God wants us bold/strong not such obvious faking.

The most insecure women brag of their strength more. "I'm a strong woman-- hear me roar"

In a post-Christian era female goddess religions emerge and lesbians become preachers.

Women's studies and ethnic studies are pseudo-disciplines and degrading quality of the real ones.

JEZEBEL SPIRIT

Jezebel can't help doing what she does, that spirit compels her to be a disgusting scuzz.

It's a spirit: Jezebel doesn't realize she's stealing, grabbing, dividing and manipulating.

Jezebel can't help saying crude things, it's spirit in her but you still must cut her loose to be king.

Jezebel can't help her grabby behavior it's weakness allowing that spirit/need the Savior.

Jezebel can't help what she does under spirit's influence but get strong so she's not a nuisance.

Jezebel spirit only gets worse until you stand against this curse coming thru women even a nurse.

Jezebel takes, meddles, gossips, divides/grabs but I want a humble maid just doing what I ask.

No logic with Jezebel. She's slippery changing the subject five times a minute so you won't know.

Since she can't be pinned down confusion keeps her on the throne so remove her then be known.

Jezebel has a secret agenda always and lies convincingly for praise and the confusion is a haze.

You can't reason with her, she never *ever* admits fault and she doesn't learn-- she's not the salt.

Even the most absurd things she obviously did she won't admit to, it's a prideful spirit too.

We've all known a Jezebel that changed our lives forever when we finally let it go/got clever.

The Jezebel seemingly rips from you your right to choose and man she really brings the blues.

Women: For you to forgive without repentance is creating a monster with you the dunce.

Jezebel gets your emotions stirred up then lets you go into a rage like she's the innocent sage.

Jezebel spirit will make you think you want her, it's actually a gut feeling of terror mislabeled in error.

The Jezebel spirit in the house from the maid made me crazy, sorry, but now it's explained.

Jezebel spirit was dormant until feminism triggered the varmint/now we're all suffering with it.

Those influenced by a Jezebel spirit always target a leader. They want all the attention and power.

The Jezebel spirit is always the victim and wants your pity. Mom makes you hate dad, shut up lady.

Maxine Waters is the Jezebel of the Hour.

When Jezebel is humble it's a religious spirit and just more trouble.

Jezebel is a self-important heretic even calling herself a "prophetess"

Simply put, Jezebel is a divider, a slighter and a Queen Bee dominator/you'll only rule without her.

Jezebel will insidiously worm into your household and you'll even love her cuz the spirit's so bold.

Jezebel is never wrong, it's always "them". Just to get on your good side she'll seemingly repent.

Don't make the Jezebel housekeeper part of your family or you'll be in divorce court speedily.

Jezebel is *never* accountable and if you ever confront she'll cry and accuse/call you a Jezebel.

Jezebel spirit looks for the hurt, wounded or insecure to become their spiritual guide/teacher.

Just when you think she's repentant an opportunity arises and she creates another terrible crisis.

Jezebel is so insidious you must eliminate the influence--don't let her back in to stay a Mrs.

Jezebel comes thru men too but a power trip comes from early rejection more often with women.

Jezebels guilt-trip calling you unChristian for not bowing to their needs--don't feel guilty, please!

Best housekeepers are invisible, humble, silent and never take sides if they want employment.

Once out, you can knock all you want broad you'll never get back in cuz we see your facade.

Jezebel twists facts/has selective memory. She's smooth, slick and convincing as her armory.

Even a court of law can't pin Jezebel down.

Jezebel wants what you have and prays "remove that person--that position belongs to me."

When you see Jezebel in your midst you must nip it in the bud or the damage will quickly erupt.

The Jezebel spirit will act in ways causing great suffering and damage along the way. Fire, today.

It isn't just your tragedy. Check out what feminists have done to you, your world and family.

Men used to love women/would never hurt em--but feminism has made em a terrible burden.

Women don't want men getting together and discussing without them there as controllers.

All liberal women hate men. Jesse Lee Peterson

They leave for college as sweet little girls and come back raving lunatics influenced by that world.

If the pastor preaches on the Jezebel spirit to scare then that spirit sure won't want to stay there.

Reactive Illness: several wives of Jezebel husbands died in their forties after abuse/suffering it.

The Jezebel spirit has claws and charisma as it gains tragic hold and attaches to intelligentsia.

In an effort to gain an indomitable footing the Jezebel spirit will attach to someone good looking.

News outlets are not about reporting news but controlling and shaping reality.

NYC will regret an evil nasty woman won, a socialist handing out free stuff. Jesse Lee Peterson

Jezebel also causes water retention. We bloat with vile insubordination esp. when paying em.

If a Jezebel Spirit's in your life you'll do absurd things and have weird dreams at night.

Your gut is terrified of this woman but magically reverses to attraction so watch out/take action.

Why are women so terrifying? It's a God-given body they're defiling and things they believe in.

Just from things they say you know they're crazy, mimicking common narrative like all mentally lazy.

It's the sweet little old ladies who are filled with heresies and will ruin your life taking their advice.

It's a bottomless pit, a dark infinite cavern--that's the godless woman and I know you've met one.

They can't help what they say, it just all pours out: the filthy cesspit of the nasty women faking clout.

She'll do anything, a nasty woman without lines. She'll turn on you too, infidelity of the unkind.

She's unstable, her moods variable. You can't trust her, the untrustworthy and unreliable.

The nasty woman goes to greatest lengths to be as nasty, filthy and disrespectful as she can be.

New women take pride in being nasty/dirty even calling themselves sex pots and having parties.

Women are the problem making anti-family/men decisions and Obama got in because of them.

Women are incapable of seeing the outcome of their lousy decisions/repeat path of destruction.

Women make decisions by how they think/feel, men make em on logic and seeing the outcome.

Men tolerate the feminist BS from a desire to be fair and have tranquility and peace at any price.

Women-hating men aren't born that way. It's adaptation to angry mama or girlfriend along the way.

Poor men are ruined by divorce: they can't see their children but still must pay child support.

Men gossip but women are ruthless/tireless. It's their whole thing, it makes their day/hell to pay.

It's true, women's scorn is worst than men's. It's due to their tenacity in getting back/irreverence.

Every woman has been lashed by a female enemy. They're assiduous, won't give up, oh my.

Danger of female enemies is their major weapon: ruthless gossip, but God hates this. Prov. 20:19

NO feminist woman is sweet, loving, tender or nurturing. Man, they believe in baby killing!

I was targeted by a feminist using gossip/unfair and felt like a cat in a room full of rocking chairs.

It was a small desert town and she managed to turn every one against me then I awoke/could see.

I was a recluse, not social. She was ultra-social, being liberal. She had the edge, I was the fool.

I'd gladly give up the vote to cut dangerous women outa politics completely, that's no joke.

Women are ruining men and children for life. With men gone world seems dark/filled with strife.

Divorce brings down a home (more than house) and the pets go to the shelter. It's so sad, a killer.

Even long term successful marriages are ended by women for the hell of it, and it's his end.

Any divorce is as terrible as it gets. Everyone suffers especially the kids and pets.

Feminism is immoral.

New women don't want men getting together without them sitting there controlling male behavior.

My experience of men is they'll do anything to keep me happy, but liberal feminists are crazy.

What made me an anti-feminist was run-ins with narcissistic women feeling blasphemed or dissed.

Feminism is ruining families and it need not be, things are beautiful if (of this falsity) we're free.

You see tiny children flipping the bird and using F-Talk, all from mama's encouragement, yuk!

All her decisions are wrong, not based on logic but false theory, feelings, empathy, virtue signaling.

They presuppose the impermanency of marriage. It's always on probation and not a good ending.

They put Johnny in therapy for wrong reasons only to be brainwashed by new age heretic legions.

A maid even tried to divide us, everyone's a feminist by default even if they think they're not.

Jezebel is so very clever she'll worm in and stay forever then you'll even say "oh well, whatever".

Wimps: The man can't do what he wants but she can do whatever she wants when she wants.

Smart women take the side of men and hate feminism.

Feminists take pride in being sluts or anything else they want. Saints have restraint/are loved.

Germany ruined by a woman. They weren't born dumb but made that way like with Mrs. Macron.

Penetrate network and your head fills up with cobwebs of "who said what to who"/screwed.

They mistake virtue signaling with virtue by taking a stand on something that is moral in nature.

Taking a moral stand they become obdurately immovable and fixed--it's women doing this.

They lecture you on false ethics and can't shut their mouth about it.

Women are the worst with false ethics when they make it politics.

Biggest contradiction in your life: girlfriend sympathizes with destructive people filled with strife.

Stop being misadvised by false Christians who are pagans and see virtue signaling as goodness.

These women are just trying to look good/have a nice image. This they call politics but it all sux.

Be a model of niceness and a nice life for those who've devolved to clutter, chaos and strife.

Fake feminists can live with contradiction because that's what they are already so I'd avoid em.

Women: vapid platitudes/childish naiveté seen as the only reality and making sure you agree.

Germany debates putting troops on streets against ISIS. This is moving fast, a female induced crisis.

Of course not all women are insane, it's a bell shaped curve. We're the edges but movin' in to serve.

The vacuity in most women is a mix of feminism, pathological altruism and not knowing anythin'

Western women are poisoned by generations of feminism.

Where women rule, feelings/emotions dominate the political landscape not reason and logic.

Weird feminist creed: Be tolerant of the intolerant.

Whatever he did to Mary his karma was Sue and now he's got me since he's paid his dues.

After rejecting patriarchy white women want meaner men and are wearing hijabs everywhere today.

Women going along with modern feminism are then pimped by it. Alex Jones

FEMINISM AND RUIN 1

What makes women so cruel is feminism and what makes em so fat is selfishness/modernism.

I loved my mother. Yes she was an alcoholic but she was old school not a liberal feminist fool.

See that little ol' lady? She's really a scorpion--get past appearances Paul said, see the inner man.

Dangerous heresies taught by lil' ol' ladies who'd do best to bake cookies cuz it's pure insanity.

Lil' old ladies saying to forgive without repentance or take in sinners who destroy our inheritance.

Dangerous heresies by lil ol' ladies aren't innocent as decisions are made/destroy irrevocably.

Meghan Markle an Obama feminist has bully pulpit for banalities, trivialities and clichés.

Meghan Markle the flashy feminist who given a chance says absolutely nothing but with class.

Could we not find Meghan fascinating with these platitudes and silly things she's been saying?

A pretty face but that's not all. Opens her mouth and it's an embarrassing virtue signaling broad.

Meghan Markle shut up it's so embarrassing these dangerous heresies and silly banalities.

Feminists seek to disprove the old Truth that sex is more important to men by sleeping around.

Feminists seeking liberation by sleeping around based on how they see men: wrong focus/death.

You got the approval of liberals and sick, drugged out cohorts/editors so now you're great?

For women it may be food, for men sex, but must tame the tiger to make gold and find success.

For men it's sex for women it's food and it's gambling for some cultures like the Asians or Jews.

You're too old to need an older catering sister. Take control now and strut your stuff faster.

She picks fights with you cuz that's what feminists do.

Women and youth are crazy but those who break through become the best, hard-workers not lazy.

Biggest contradiction of all time: Feminists going for Jihadis, sick of the wimpy nothing soyboys.

And the sex sins--little kids instructed in school, just think of this and ask them if they're cool.

Cinderella: The template is two against one so become the queen or recreate this/stay down.

Low IQ pops come here play video games live on dole but they're real men so women love em.

Feminists who've battled husbands or ruined them in divorce have fallen for Jihadis of course.

Omarosa: We all know a person who will turn on you cannot be trusted. Traitors are hated by both sides, busted.

Women aren't held back by men as feminists suggest. It's not patriarchy it's brain mass.

They disparage/trash women of substance while they laud a porn queen: that's the liberal scene.

Girly men aren't innocent if they gossip like a girl so don't trust em, male feminists are sadists.

Don't believe what mom says about dad or what he says about her. Go to that person, hear?

Don't listen to mom about dad cuz that's her feelings not yours, judge for yourself after divorce.

Don't listen to mom/dad about your crazy uncle/aunt either. Genius/saints are hated tho' clever.

If mom/dad are liberal they hate conservative aunt/uncle so make your own decisions if able.

Was your aunt hated as a conservative or sinner? For you could have learned stuff from her.

God is within so everything you're looking for is already there, but you forgot distracted by glare.

He never beat her up nor had an affair. But to hear her talk you'd think he was a sadist I declare.

Mother wasn't a raving harridan but submissive and sweet, looked much better/able to think.

How funny: Angry, fat, ugly feminists saying men are raping em when all they want is to escape em.

Vindictive women taking advantage of the social climate and pinning men with things/ruining them.

Women love girlie men (more controllable) and that's why they loved Obama despite being a dictator.

Barrack Obama was a feminist and look what happened to the country: he almost finished it.

Trump is the forgotten man from the fifties core--that's why we love him: we don't have it anymore.

They loved the girlie man (fake tears) Obama who tried to destroy the country of America.

The perfect Order of God: God in Christ, Christ in man, man over woman, woman over children.

Barbaric terrorist refugees are hot items with Swedish gals after their men became cucks and fell.

Problem is the women's vote. They took men way, gov. is husband--that's all they want.

Women are spoiled by spineless girlie men so go wild with anger/regression with the real man.

They aren't used to real man, calling em animals--they've been spoiled by girlie men they know.

Men are to be head of their wives (not "household"). But even preachers are afraid to be bold.

Even strong men are terrified of their wives saying "God rules her" rather than "I rule"/terror.

Even preachers are controlled by wives (tho' they play a role)--not children of God as foretold.

I have never met such pansies: men terrified of women. It's sickening not just wimpy/we hate em.

Men are to rule women but modernity makes that thought a trigger of contention with woman.

If he rules her she'll get all her friends against him then they gossip/mis-advise to get rid of him.

Men: If you don't man-up they'll take the manhood out of you for good.

Absent fathers/brought up by liberal mothers = catastrophe: girlie men or women who are angry.

Black preachers supporting everything wrong: controlling wives and Black Lives Matter/strife.

Feminists use rejection/discord as a rudder to control systems and they pass this onto sons.

Feminists/liberals hate white, straight, hetero Christian males who are becoming girlie, cucked, frail.

When feminism gets in a woman's system she starts bitchin'

Marrying a prince is marrying into patriarchy. It's amazing any "feminist" would do that, malarkey.

Feminists hating men are going crazy over Trump cuz he's the epitome of what a great man is, luv'.

As he plowed thru the vicious crowd trying to kill em she said "aren't you gonna try to *help* him?"

Women have it so badly turned around it's a wonder we're still here after they got vote/took over.

If you don't know principals (property) you vote BIG GOV and socialism via virtue signaling.

Would feminists ever admit gender inequality doesn't exist? No cuz it doesn't suit their interests.

Moreover, look at the poor women in other countries then tell me your troubles honey.

Not only do women control men thru sex, they ruin the lives of their ex.

When women control men thru sex it's not sexism, but when men do it it is? This is typical bias.

What does feminist Meghan say about the spiking of female genital mutilation in the UK?

Feminist in name only: I'm all for equality but I'm marrying into royalty.

Me Too: all jumping on bandwagon saying they were raped--watch for false charges and escape.

FEMINISM AND RUIN 1

Advised by a shady liberal feminist to divorce she ruined and devastated her life of course.

She/he's trying to tell you white is black and you're going along with it?

Women are idiots when it comes to politics. Open borders, gov. tyranny--these are facts, look at stats.

If women don't know principals they succumb to shallow surface emotionality, prey to drama.

Worldwide, women know less about politics than men and aren't up with current affairs, just friends.

Regardless of "gender equality" women know less than men about politics, it's just a fact.

Women repeatedly vote against own interests and don't know it, virtue signalers easily molded.

The more privileges a woman has the less she knows about politics. Less gender gap = social/gossip.

The more "equality" she gets the less she knows about politics--I just can't get over that.

You'd think increased female presence in politics would bring kindness not killing and ruthlessness.

In high IQ areas there are only men, not women--these female deficiencies are blamed on men.

It's a huge problem: the more power women get the less they know.

Women are so vastly uninformed yet arrogant about their opinions since it's all virtue signaling.

Women are significantly uninformed compared to men and thus female genius has no friends.

Scary: women are voting but are FAR less informed than men (see stats friends),

Women are less informed and vote left. Test me on this: sit down and talk with her about politics.

People are surprised I would take men's side--that's a sign identity is all and logic is gone.

Some women are logical--those who break thru become the best: smart, spiritual and practical.

Their answer like reflex: The problem is not that women are uninformed but that men are sexist.

A pernicious lie: "Men privileged, women oppressed. Hire, promote and reward accordingly".

Do not give women power over sexuality. Stefan Molyneux

Never pay her bills cuz she's sleeping with you--that's paying for sex and devalues her too.

Never date a woman if she's trashy, empty, shallow or useless. Just turn away, no need to address.

Science shows women feel far more pain than men so don't send em to war if you're their friend.

Women vote for bigger government esp. single moms, they see it as security and protection.

Married women go conservative since they don't want state to take the stuff the husband built up.

Creeping socialism in the west, massive emotionality, uninformed women on a worldwide scale.

In Sweden, voicing an opinion saying there are men vs. women can truly bring you opprobrium.

Destroying gender roles is the major way they weaken society along with the migrant tsunami.

She may be smart but what she needs is education of the heart.

Build him UP don't tear him down cuz it's only gonna hurt you in the end making him a clown

If Hillary'd gotten in all women would *feel* president and woulda made hell on earth for husbands.

Grace Jones is another woman who says nothing. Be a mystery not flashy but so embarrassing.

She's older, divorced, an actress and a feminist--Poor Harry, she'll control him, that's how this is.

The new trend: men going for older moms, that's what they want in relationships now: wow.

Bullying create hermits and emotional damage. The worst bullies are women = lifelong baggage.

Learn to cook then get any man because they're so sick of feminists who couldn't care less.

No events, I just wanna enjoy all my moments in the home thank you

You want me to go where, when it's so inferior/boring compared to my own home? Oh come on...

They're all sick powerless people looking for other people to control.

Not raised by dad but mom who makes her hate him/all men she's suspicious of every little thing.

You can take down a country thru war and pestilence or thru rank and uninformed sentimentality.

Once committed to immorality it's nearly impossible to change course.

I don't hate Hillary I just wanna see justice done and I despise her doings, is that so offensive?

He calls his wife "Mama" and she treats him like a baby. Is this pathetic, what do you think?

For Life of the Mother abortion is justified 2% of the time but used as an excuse 98% of the time.

These liberals/globalists are so sick they call baby killing (abortion) and child rape "freedom".

Taught to be social and loving a fake personna took over and masochism-- letting people in.

A nation without dads raised by feminist twits should love their strong leader but it's the opposite.

People hated my husband for the same reason: disciplinarian, military man, gets the job done.

A nation of twits and cucks hate the true man since feminists and liberals call it an anachronism.

The true man is blessed by God to lead his family. If the woman fights that, wow what treachery.

When enontiodromia (system inversion) occurs you can't believe you were intimidated by her.

When momma ain't happy no one is but why does it have to be constant just cuz she's feminist?

Hate Trump? He's the strong man daddy you never had, raised by mom who made you resent that.

He's the strong dad, something we never had. Wimpy men allowed their strength to be denigrated.

They hate Trump cuz mommy made em hate daddy then feminists said men are evil and shady.

Look at the insanity of female leaders, letting floods of people in to wreak havoc on their peoples.

Liberal feminized men hangout with females not out of interest/love but it's all they'd have.

It's not so much women vote thru emotion but phony virtue signaling for temporary thrill of ego.

They wanna put the whole blame on men who are mild and rational compared to women.

They're sluts and proud of it, primed in the schools saying if you don't you're repressed/not legit.

The feminist thing is harsh in women as they fight with each other in a minute (female pugilism).

They hold each other down like crabs in a bucket. Genius blocked by female community of suckups.

Feminist gig is wildly weak without knowing it. Witches, bitches, raving maniacs out to get president.

Liberal feminized men hangout with females not out of interest or love but it's all they got.

A disloyal generation contradicts you. She expects to love your enemies and have you too.

Saw a picture of a dead child on the beach so millions were let in to kill, destroy and rape.

She's the kind who forgives by running to your enemies and spilling the beans to please.

See that sweet little old lady there, she's really a scorpion. See past images, that's maturation.

Little old lady bakes cookies/seems so sweet but can cause so much trouble you're up a creek.

Of course the scorpion's gonna act like a kitten that's the whole thing while they're manipulatin'

A family of mostly women chooses one victim and when he dies another is chosen: scapegoatism.

Don't think a little old lady is harmless and can't cause trouble: they've lived/smart, double.

If you criticize her behavior it means you don't like her: refusing correction marks the immature.

Men aren't catcalling ugly women with purple armpit hair who swear so stop you false accusers.

All feminists have an anecdote about the horrible cruelty of men but men are nice, it's THEM.

All men are sinners that includes sweet little old ladies too: we all gotta repent, that's the truth.

Art is to uplift, show us what God is, thru beauty feel bliss--not this s--t by liberal twits.

Going around acting tough, who are you kidding it's just media fluff and we've had enough.

As an enabler she "can forgive anything" then puts you down because you draw the line.

Justin Trudeau's a globalist puppet taking mother and father outa all docs and you like this idiot?

Globalists have mobilized feminists to destroy the family unit and the father is **KEY**: the head.

Incompetent, dullard or mean mean are role models. It's in all the ads and confirmed in schools.

The feminists have been burned by men/hate all men and our answer is to embrace **REAL** men.

Men victimized in divorce court and no-consent abortions: Father's rights are nil, an abomination.

Dad your role is most important and don't let man-hating feminists tell you otherwise/evil disguised.

Liberals love to diminish the role of fathers and compare it to the saintly mother but dad is head!

They put down fatherhood because it is masculinity, their only defense against enemies.

Illuminating: The lady on the left wants to make everything look nice and refuses to criticize.

Women can't replace men and dad was the gentle loving one while mom was a raving harridan.

Women are inferior thinkers without logic or presence but those who break thru become the best.

Women have poor character cuz it takes strength to restrain from greed and that's the arbiter.

She couldn't resist what she did cuz she is what she is—the wicked never question their wants, sis.

A Man is created in the image of God: righteous, unafraid of adversity, protective of family.

Masculinity is destroyed but also femininity: sweet little ladies not tattooed freaks so shady.

Both genders are being destroyed, eaten up in a big blob empty vortex of crude blandness.

My so-called friend (feminist) would always befriend my enemies. We gotta choose sides, see?

They think they can have things both ways--it's doublethink saying it's ok to be contradictory.

They can't help it, if acting that way it's demons and unthinking reflexive actions/good riddance.

It's always about what's good for them not what's right.

You're not yourself, you're MOM for we become who we're angry at. Forgive/be released/be glad.

How low the left goes: Ivanka can't be a feminist wearing heals and a pink dress let alone a bow.

Women belong in the home and you can't get me out of it while few get in: home maintenance.

Man is to be over the women but in most homes he's under her domination = demons.

Liberals are big in making up stuff and calling it spiritual when it's occult and the end is miserable.

Feminism warps the minds of females and blocks interest with males and thus birth rate fails.

Feminists are against beauty pageants as dehumanizing but not pornography? Fascinating.

Those behind feminism/pornography are the same--both wannna destroy the west by what they say.

Feminists want to pull down beauty and pornographers treat beautiful women like whores, see.

Stupid liberal female politicians over Germany, UK, Scotland and Wales: an experiment to fail.

I know by looking at her. Can you really know a book from it's cover? Yes it's easy/can't love her.

They are indistinguishable from each other and claim something they are not, birds of a feather.

It is so necessary for female psyche to feel virtuous and loving they willingly let in the enemy.

Pathological altruism/empty virtue signaling combined with social equals women, what a shame.

Leader females: could they be dishonest, communist, globalist, socialist open border shills?

Image degraded by so many words of lengthy explanations from inflated self-importance.

Female politicians have no morals and seek to eradicate cultural values, they are of no use.

Esprit de corps: need family cuz a nation without fathers raised by liberal mothers made us empty.

Signaling virtue but into pornography and acting out too--contradictions of modern females.

Since body is endlessly mutable why not control it totally though feminists call it unacceptable?

Why no morals? Cuz they're liberals who think they're good and true morality misunderstood.

True morality is what God said not what you want, desire or prefer to believe.

I'd gladly give up mine to block female vote cuz what they foolishly choose is a fact/STAT.

Fools/female politicians love to hear applause when signaling their virtue and it's self-reinforcing.

That female ego beams with the audience applause and it's so sickening a contradiction.

FEMINISM AND RUIN 2
Holding Women Down like Crabs in a Barrel

Main liberal shove-down: We're all Equal: *ONE*.

Main cosmology shove-down since kindergarten: we're all ONE (equal) and thus this violence hon'. We can't have a mass belief in egalitarianism when science clearly shows clear differentials. It's egalitarian orthodoxy that science rejects--that we're all the same, a myth so lame. So tell them--If you won't lead em, who will? Now get in gear, it's not just about you. In times of chaos only he who states things simply wins. Women with keen intellect who break thru the pugnacious feminist haze become best, I'm amazed. What is needed to return to sanity is the return of patriarchy and rise of conservative society. We need men to protect us baby.

Written and Illustrated by
Karen Kellock Ph.D.

They were raised by their liberal democrat mammas so they reflect her not the dad for balance.

Men tend to follow principals in politics, women not: it's all about emotion as the nation rots.

If the husband loves God even more than her she will never leave him/only him she'll adore.

Men know women go wrong but are too weak to confront them—you're supposed to be the head, man.

Wimpy men could never truly be a friend to women it's just mutual feelings of persecution.

I appreciate how you wanna share the burden by telling me all that stuff but please shut up.

Think of all the women needing self-forgiveness for abortion--hating self, life, being an ex-mom.

Diet restrictions are unnecessary hell. Eat what you want then don't eat to tomorrow = swell.

Obesity is not female empowerment just sickening.

If a woman can cook she has it made. It makes a home and they'll love her truly, no charades.

Gender dysphorics are deranged symptoms of a general social decline who do deserve this.

Any man who says he's a liberal is a woman. Jesse Lee Peterson

It gives em a thrill to virtue signal and be good. They don't care about the high cost, understood?

Feminists have been in control for so long they can't accept a real man in there so they hate him.

Feminism represents evil for last fifty years so it should be interesting now a real man is here.

Feminists have been all for killing babies and women having sex with the neighbor lady--shady!

God works thru man to woman so evil wants men to be women, the worst thing for everyone.

Mothers destroy sons (under guise of helping em) by hating the father or anger from ancestors.

Feminism destroyed families by degrading the conduit of God: thru Dad came God's reality.

Her mom turned her away from her father so now she hates all men and makes her son hate him.

Fatherless boys become Satan's toys cuz they lost their rudder and can't win in encounters.

Everything is in reverse. Weak men following wives around like boys or puppies or worse.

Two celebrity hangings in one week both connected to Hillary Clinton--what are we to think?

Fatherless females hate men, masculinity, discipline. Logic gone too since that comes from dad.

Fatherless females are like a rudderless ship and tend to promiscuity for a feeling of kinship.

Dad teaches restraint (don't hit girls) and brings focus, logic, reason, future vision to our world.

Dad just wants to be: tranquility in a happy home with thee. But feminism is divisive, you see?

A Man is different from a girlie girl, soyboy, beta male, gigolo or a liberal.

How are you a Man when you voted for everything a godless liberal female would like abortion?

In the fifties women were sweet little ladies and all were happy but now they're harridans/raving.

Natalism: Culture centered on the children but feminist anti-natalists die in the historical dustbin.

Equal outcomes is the highest virtue of a feminized society but brings such devastation, oh my.

Feminism disincentivizes men.

Woman from fatherless home will hate masculine authority and mimic her harridan mommy.

Mom is ANGRY and makes you hate dad, all men and life since she ruined homelife thru strife.

Why is mom so angry? Because she's alone, has to do it all, no REAL home/no one really cares.

What is an insane asylum: a home with kids (and pets) raised by liberal feminist moms.

Had a wonderful marriage, family/home and brought it down encouraged by feminism all around.

Feminist moms encourage terrible things like homos, masturbation even abortion: abominations!

Feminist moms are terrible teachers of debauchery and disgusting past times like Harry Potter.

Crazy neurotic female brings down her own house. She's even happy being alone/dating a louse.

It's exciting and wonderful to create a home. It's the most superior job and has great rewards.

To think judges give mom custody when dad could inject some sensible reality/we'd be happy.

Even grandmothers use "F" talk, anxious to be accepted by younger folk. Disgusting, grow up.

Dad can't see the kids, she wants full control. That's the way all liberals are when reason's gone.

Men are nationalists (reason), women are globalists (controlled, bought, emotions are the gist).

Trudeau put mostly females on his cabinet to be "fair" with "equal outcome"--Canada's done.

God over man, man over woman, woman over children: Good men brings discipline/happy home.

Bad men are not the head of their wives nor bring love and order into the family: unhappiness.

Feminist moms are WRONG on every single thing yet allowed to raise children to be insane.

Feminists hate all men, masculinity, logic, reason and approaching all problems the same.

Women are lawless: they want each situation approached by their many justifications/excuses.

Female geniuses are totally obstructed in female culture and end up with men as their nurturers.

Fake liberal tears over border babies when they could care less about separated prison families.

Rachel Maddow fake tears over border kids--never mind about daily murders in abortion mills.

Liberals don't care about babies they want power and wealth and to make us bend by any means.

Maintain your home reality at all costs. All help must melt in and not interrupt one bit, Boss.

She has too big of an ego to see how glad you are to be rid of her so just enjoy your reward dear.

Men rule by laws but women by excuses, justifications and a million words that are so boring.

Women were denied the vote due to emotional decisions not what's right and we see their spite.

The logorrhea of the self-justifier is an endless barrage and you must not give in: manage it.

Fatherless females are emotionally insecure so create laws that are so wrong for our culture.

The evil spirit in the house makes you think you want it but don't invert reality: just FACE it!

Angry women can't love: children of the lie.

Demon in the house: we mal-adapt by needing it more but enjoying it less until we see her DIS.

Women like Clinton who believe in abortion to the 9th month quoting the bible: despicable.

They're not thinking for themselves and that's why this is happening.

Now that she/he's gone I see it was a demon causing our aneurisms which are disappearing.

Feminists are cowards, they can't take the heat. Pin them down and they'll deny they cheat.

Tell em what they did wrong then a million excuses/they can't be pinned down. Slippery, I'm done.

Her endless bitching caused his aneurism cuz men **ARE** sensitive to their environment, ma'am.

Dad draws lines: don't hit girls, don't steal, don't even touch what isn't yours and life will be swell.

I was an angry woman but then realized I was lied to and got over it.

Jesse was an angry black but then realized he'd been lied to, and got over it.

Evil is angry and blaming other people. It's either evil or good: black hood.

You've been brainwashed to be angry, and lesbians and transgenders aren't real women.

Angry women have been lied to/bought the lie totally. Tho' a wrong premise there goes the energy.

She's focused on revenge and what a tragedy it's a woman's infinite dark wrath, and all that.

Maxine Waters is inciting mob violence and it's extremely serious, dangerous, treasonous.

Maniacal Maxine Waters, Mob Instigator

Is that a strong women yelling like a hyena? Making demands and trying to fool ya?

Flaring up at criticism is very female and men do it now, raised by moms who hate males.

Neurotic females resent their mothers then become them but forgiveness opens em up again.

Legalistic liberal female very angry not a strong person but watch out baby.

She's always playing victim like she has it bad and you're the cad, just say good riddance man.

Her kids after being around her weak character act disrespectfully, even violent mal-adaptors.

Raised by mom who hates men now. Resents her but becomes her 'til forgiveness bestowed.

What you permit you promote, what you allow you encourage, what you condone you own. Michelle Malkin

We become what we hate, so tho' he's sick of the bitchin' he thinks like Mama and becomes gay.

NOT ALL but most women under fifty are out of control and very immoral. Jesse Lee Peterson

Girlie men: To defy a demanding feminist woman is to say "no" to mama, so they give in.

You being a "male feminist" is a dead giveaway of your treachery to truth/it's liberal chicanery.

Jezebel can't help acting like a total jerk it's a matter of the spirit inside her.

I see what you're up against. A wild, foolish, gullible, group-driven little witch who's also a snitch.

Jezebel can't help being divisive, snide, backbiting, attention-demanding or manipulating.

Pussy hat women's marches are all for open borders, crazy witches.

She's not a backstabber it's the spirit within her but you still gotta cut her lose or bye bye future.

Female heretics--crazy women--confirm bad men calling it "forgiving" but it's w/out repentance.

Just because she's a little ol' lady doesn't mean she's not a heretic who can lead you up a creek.

There's such a thing as a Jezebel spirit and it comes thru male or female and is very treacherous.

The foolish female fawned over the wrong group-determined narrative and ended your marriage.

Anger went away when I forgave mommy cuz we always become who we resent/ain't it funny.

Woman belongs in her home. I could never go out there again, chemical pea soup of Babylon.

Jealous people try to get her away from home since that's her protection-- refuse that direction.

They want me on their turf to compete. Not happy as a bee in my own walled territory in full glory.

Women don't know what they're missing not staying home, It's the only part of world we control.

Real men aren't liberals, only beta males are like those.

Mean-spirited Jezebel will add fuel to the fire. Once she knows your weakness she's a liar.

If Jezebel hears you're a jealous woman she'll stir things up to really incur that emotion/rub it in.

Everything is just the way I want it in my home, like climate control, warm not cold.

Due to feminism women have become pugnacious and it's reflected in mean spirited politics.

Jezebel is an insidious divider. She insinuates, mutters and points to make sure you hear her.

She witched so much against Trump now we all hate her. As usual they overreach with bad behavior.

Maxine never gets anything done but run her extremely wide bass-fish mouth. Donald Trump

The Jezebel Scare: She won't let anything stop her, is manipulative and interferes everywhere.

The Maxine Waters democrat fringe will effectively turn dems into republicans. Donald Trump

Jezebel: Suddenly she wrenches away all of your Self Will--not thinking anything of it, too.

You hired her, not the other way around. So who is she to block your will or be so fowl?

A Jezebel spirit makes you think you need her and it's very depressing but good to fear her.

Bifurcation: Everything splits into male or female. Even with homos one is always passive you know.

Men and women: natural partners or natural enemies? Mutually dependent all minutes of day.

Hurts to see spouse isn't with God.

The raging spirit of Jezebel is happening now with the manipulations of global control.

A backstabbing loudmouth liar (no matter their color) is a dog but I'd prefer not to insult dogs.

Jezebel spirit divides marriages, families, churches and nations--a splinter factor/abomination.

Greedy overreach marks the leech.

Only remedy for Jezebel spirit destroying your life, home and nation: Don't get involved, avoid em.

Men are told the pathway to virtue is weakness and harmlessness, a most dangerous myth.

Liberalism is actually the spirits of antichrist and Jezebel, spirits of division and discord.

The new maid is humble and causes no trouble, the other one ran rampant telling all to the rabble.

If weak in sin demons flow in and like the Jezebel spirit you'll be compelled to meddle, divide, gossip.

Jezebel is playing you like a fiddle. She knows your triggers and Achilles heel so good riddance.

Question: Did God make man for the man, or did God make woman for the man? What is God sayin?

She knew your weak points cuz you told her, she couldn't resist getting you outa joint so drop her.

Good heavens what's gonna happen now that witch is running

I wanna strong man not a girlie man or a beta male or a mama's boy or especially a silly liberal.

Women let him think he's in control when he's not--women are cunning and kids are screwed up.

Women are cunning, knowing broaching a subject directs his mind in the direction she's intending.

Get him thinking her way, drop subtle hints into mix, goad him here/there then give him credits.

Yelling won't work. Keep sweet and be smart then it's a smooth ride not a rocky road/curse.

Women want equality so yell to get it then he becomes sheepish/bubbling with anger beneath it.

Wise women know it's all in the approach. If on the attack he holds back so drop hints with tact.

Controlling man thru sex is witchcraft. She's a deep cavern/bottomless pit with daggers: fact

Mind like a steel trap and articulate ability to tear him down with facts, that's the feminist axe.

She tears him down, he grovels to get her back. From his low position she looks good Mack.

Since it's based on false narrative/virtue signaling they rail at husbands who just wanna please em.

She's not tough and strong she's angry and resentful. See the difference or life becomes miserable.

Women more articulate with steel-trap minds so easily break him down in a fight, until the violence.

They're so hypnotized by feminists they rail at husbands without letup and you KNOW THIS.

Quibble over words and it muddles the waters. Pin em down, can't be done on what matters.

Unless wife becomes a sweet little lady it's gonna be shady or he'll fall into girlie man or soyboy.

It's not manly to talk so much, you were raised by your mother (women are loquacious brother).

Not since the sweet lil' ladies in the fifties were they worth a dime but are destructive all the time.

Spirit: It all comes down to Jezebel IN her and it means horror, alienation, guilt and fear.

Her spirit: It all comes down to Jezebel IN her and it means horror, alienation, guilt and fear.

The Jezebel spirit is always implicitly man-hating. Are you kidding? She hates your good men.

Jezebel puts down your husband or insinuates you're under his control as the dominant one: Hah!

Don't waste energy in social spread but focus all of it inside--a home of nooks/crannies so fine.

Much of what we see now is not Christianity but communism with virtue signaling.

Women were home-centered but now it's all about going out and home-life has suffered a lot.

She always wants to go out/can't stand staying home so the dishes pile up and it's hardly like Rome.

Being angry and resentful she can't take it out on him (he's gone) so the axe falls on the children.

When she gets upper hand she wrenches all self-will from you and thus good marriages are few.

If you want a wife look for one who is traditional and strong enough to submit to a man to cuddle.

Liberal acts like a petulant child cuz father was absent, mother was angry and God defiled.

Love him like a little boy and he'll become a man because he can finally trust/love someone.

Matriarchal societies in times of cultural decay when the men are cuckholded and say "whatever, ok".

Matriarchal societies during cultural decay when the men are cuckholded and say "whatever, ok".

As women become macho and men girlie men relationships don't work cuz women don't like em.

As boys, couldn't deal with mama then marries fem and hell breaks loose repeating early trauma.

Liberal feminists hate men, more as they regress into cuckholded beta males and it's sad.

When you break down the family you open the door to evil. It's happened to black now white people.

You can talk against men forever but not one word about the female's role in violence or whatever.

It was a Greek tragedy between sisters and things got so bad as the FEAR drove em all mad.

Liberal women hate men, turn children against fathers & don't love what's right or brings honors.

A woman can lie and a man goes to jail.

Pass laws protecting women from men but none protecting men from women acting like vermin.

Every law they pass is against family and men yet we're not allowed to talk about this hellish den.

Women who love men--fathers/sons--see the truth about persecution of males/women have won.

Women won't admit to being a psycho B from hell but many act this out--does this ring a bell?

Women blame men for the worst stereotype of that gender--being violent against her or whatever.

Women are now inviolate, you can't bring any of this up--only the most courageous talk about it.

Women think it's cute to get back at men for "centuries of abuse" like it's victory for all of em too.

Female ego won't allow em to admit to this or to fess up and overcome it so it gets worse, see it?

Since mom was a raving lunatic I just figured it was comic and emulated it until I woke up.

Women have been given permission to be a Psycho B so proudly/blatantly act it out guilt-free.

What stopped me from being a psycho B was marrying a military man and then I was free.

Wow--women are slapping men in public and they even think it's cute to be so violent. Wake up!

When women slap men they don't expect to be slapped back and if he does he goes to jail: fact.

The more she gets from him the more she wants it: love, reassurance but then the violence.

She starts the fights if he isn't paying enough attention to her at night or any perceived slight.

It's a female demon that makes her out of control and in this era it's confirmed/rewarded you know.

Signs of a sick relationship: When you're with him, no pain. When not, feelings of torture again.

After getting all her love needs met, when he's gone that's when the real craziness starts I'll bet.

Fears of abandonment take over and she acts needy towards him, a huge turn off bringing rejection.

Without him she's alone with her thoughts--an endless tirade of insults seen as all his fault.

When alone she hates herself so then condemns him for it since that's the current narrative.

Women have been blowing up for decades and tho' it's no-fault to them the men will walk away.

Her thoughts are from her past which she thinks has all to do with him so he's endlessly sassed.

Women can overcome being a raving lunatic psycho B but first they have to wake up and see it.

Female demons even turn on their friends and if you've ever experienced this you know it man.

When they inevitably split up she thinks it's all his fault and won't accept any of it--what a nut.

After the split he tells of her lunacy and she says "it's all onesided--has nothing to do with me."

The woman's place is being the man's helpmeet but now it's all about meeting her own needs.

She never notices her contribution to the situation or crazy way she acted always blaming him.

If she doesn't accept her place and keep sweet she reverts to the other extreme in a dead heat.

A woman can grow up today simply by seeing the part she played.

Pray to God for forgiveness for acting like mother who you resented so you acted just like her.

Forgive by seeing what's driving them--for it's not them but this thing making a home in them.

To forgive her see the early trauma in her life making her a monster full of strife, and what a relief.

Domestic violence is most always pinned on men but never the woman who triggers it, amen?

Now is the time to turn the children back to their fathers if you can get past the abusive mothers.

Satan is doing all he can to put out the light of fathers as world goes to hell/only God can solve it.

We're taught in media/schools how males are evil/violent and men are so weak they go along with it.

I've noticed how women start the violence and men respond to it. Women should fess up you twits.

Having been taught it's all men's fault she sleuths to find more reasons to hate his guts.

Bitchiness/argumentativeness is a form of domestic violence.

Bitchiness starts the violence so keep sweet for happiness.

When men verbally abuse it's domestic violence but when women rail like a maniac, not a chance.

When a man finally meets a sweet woman he can't believe what he's missed after that vermin.

Women act as though he walloped her for nothing and it's confirmed by all movies and sitcoms.

Just the way you're talking in your comments proves the point of the female's verbal violence.

Caution: Mama's ornery today and everyone knows no one's happy when she gets that way.

Shoving, pushing, needling, falsely accusing and articulately tearing him down without mercy.

Women hate it when we generalize, they want a tedious case-by-case and never apologize.

Real women are not threatened by this info: they've either repented or see it all around ya know.

You cannot say what women do to men.

He can be yelling and if she smacks him she gets away with it but if he smacks her it's prison.

With booze it's an atom bomb in the house especially when her fem friends see him as a louse

70% of divorces are wife initiated but how much was because her fem friends encouraged it?

Rarely do violent females go to jail but the male is automatically assumed guilty without fail.

Women jealous of men's "power position" seek to make things happen to ruin that tradition.

Godless/liberal/feminist women hate men so be honest about this so we can turn it all around.

Brainwashed with lies, men agree or are quiet about it and generations are suffering from it.

Though evil exists in both sexes it's not true what they've said about men so forgive you ex's.

For the most part women start the violence and men respond. Jesse Lee Peterson

Men represent Christ on earth for woman so must learn never to let HER push him to be a lemon.

Can't be logical with her always bringing up the dead past until what the hell you smack her.

FEMINISM AND RUIN 2

Satan put women in positions of power while also restricting criticism and making men cower.

Myth: men are mean to women. Solution: pass laws so she can even lie and he goes to prison.

Things get so heated and he's no match with words so what's left to do but smack the girl.

Keep sweet, shut up, overlook, let things pass and love him like a child who needs you, lass.

Feminism originated to destroy the family not help women. They were happy in the home, nappin.

Good women are against male-bashing just as much as men for families are destroyed therein.

Women need men, men need families and children need fathers and mothers.

Criticizing women will have the FBI at your door. It happens and with time it's happening more.

It started with the female vote. Men would never approve gay marriage or teaching tiny kids smut.

It's set up in such an emotional (female) way it makes you look bad if you don't think it's all-ok.

Husband said "I can't make her stop drinking or I'll go to jail" so let her kill herself/family go to hell.

Men represent Christ on earth for woman so she must learn to never push him to be a lemon.

Women have power over a man so why not use it to encourage him? What are his talents, ask him.

Laws: women are protected from men but not men protected from women and murder's happening.

How can coed sports be equal opportunity for the girl? And yet women push it in this crazy world.

In coed sports they soften the boys down to not compete so tough with girls, destroying them more.

Strong family = strong society, weak family = weak society--and globalists know that unfortunately.

Marrying a military career man cured my prickly orneriness real quick and I was glad he did.

Female anger from unresolved conflict or uncompleted mourning seeps out in incremental bitching.

What modern women don't understand: a good man and having children is most fulfilling/gone.

Silly feminists are pawns of globalists--due to the bad influence they've been successful at this.

When men are lost they tolerate crazy women more, hanging on but things get worse with her.

Turn hearts back to fathers. The beta males, soyboys or girlie men were raised by their mothers.

Men are always apologizing I've noticed and it's because they've adapted to an angry feminist.

After an angry mother/two sisters and belligerent female friends I know very well what this is.

Women are supposed to be keepers of the hearth: Keep bad out and educate morals in youth.

Blacks and women: If they can keep you angry they can control you.

Good women are against male-bashing just as much as men, for families are destroyed therein.

Racism does not exist, it's a made-up word. Sexism either, men really used to want you girls!

I dare you to show **ONE TWEET** proving Trump is a racist, these are lies of evil liberals/feminists.

Fathers not around, raised by angry mothers then the big lie is completed by the race hustlers.

Keeping blacks angry separates their soul from God so they'll become unproductive/more mad.

Feminism is a false religion and the results on the female personality are really devastatin'

Finding a good woman is harder than finding a ruby in a haystack (or something like that).

As women take over churches the whole set up has changed. It's just new age crap and deranged.

Going against her natural/decent inclinations to refuse sex to the uncommitted she gets mad.

A "MAN" loves what is right with his heart soul and might and leads the way, ready to fight.

The Man is to be the head of his wife but liberals will never agree with that despite the strife.

Two thirds of colleges are women only cuz society caters to them--liberals are holding back men.

Ask em if the man is to be the head of the wife--they all balk, change the subject, mock or deny it.

Women use law enforcement as sidekick strong arm, the enforcer of venom against husbands.

Women love Al-Anon for an audience of diatribe against husbands, a gossip mill, venom land.

False accusation charges: the Domestic Abuse Business and the Child Molestation Business.

The whole system and every sub-department is geared up and dug in against men: see it friends.

Lost in the confusion of false accusation innocent men are put away every day, every hour hon'

Men are Christ on earth yet condemned by vindictive women in cahoots with law enforcement.

Vindictive woman is cheered on by friends and since she's geared to be social it brings her grin.

Judicial system hates men as well. Screw-men business is huge/movies confirm he's guilty as hell.

Men: No fathers/raised by angry mothers then marry angry wives who take em to the cleaners.

Wife wins good image (victim) with legal on her side with kids too and he's sunk/can't say a thing.

Why do so many men go against men/take her side? Without knowing details/to be seen as nice.

A man is not a liberal and any man who says he's a liberal is a woman. Jesse Lee Peterson

The liberal man thinks like a woman and calls the decent conservative "racist"

Since women don't know anything but slogans they use "racist" as rudder to control conversations.

Liberal men are cuckholded and immoral, they think like women and could NEVER protect y'all.

They act like the only differences between male and female is physical. WOW, it's fantastic/infinite.

The difference between the two sexes is so infinite and that's why we say "vive la différence"!

The poison of hate, blame and victimhood has destroyed their willingness to be godly and good.

Even churches have become liberal social clubs because women took over and you know what.

We have the classiest first lady yet liberals drag her down to the gutter as something shady.

The FLOTUS is stately and regal not an emotional wasteland of falderal.

"Just too dam bad about you" said mom the shrew and then I mimicked her 'til neurosis was through.

How telling, men's clubs of America all love the man. Shriners, Masons--they all love Trump.

2nd wave feminism/Gloria Steinem killed men's clubs so they ended up in strip clubs, thanks a lot.

MEN NEED women-free zones. These witches just wanna end good fun and of course control.

If the most beautiful women are men why can't we do it too friends?

I'd hate an argument with Whoopi or the other dames. I've had enough cat fights with the lame.

Like most women without information/debating tools, Whoopi lost it/went ballistic like a fool.

WOMEN: it's just easier for them to go with the emotional talking points and the facts be damned.

Women with keen intellect who break thru the pugnacious feminist haze become best, I'm amazed.

Outside of the home it's all social adaptation but when inside it's fun, relaxation and creation.

Feminism ruined so many great marriages. Kids and pets lost their homes too/so unfortunate.

If someone's pedophiliac it doesn't mean they act on it but it's still too much for most spouses.

Judge Jeanine is breaking new ground with this, we've all been a sad victim of liberal feminists.

Liberals play so dirty and they'll hurt thee.

Immigration at it's core is to benefit those already in the country. Floods of unvetted groups, oh baby.

Dictator Obama: social transformation without representation.

The View was weaponized disinformation to keep women dumb.

Crazed liberal females are vulgar and disgusting: "Get outa my behind and my vagina" says Whoopi.

Deranged lunatic Whoopi Goldberg thinks she speaks for all women but she doesn't/she is vermin.

Be sure before asking God to make it happen, it may invite predation.

Women divorce the men and it's mostly based on false accusation--it's Big Business to get em.

How do race hustlers get power and wealth? By yelling "racist" that's how

Pope washes feet of a wishy washy globalist view of Islam.

Just pull the plug they'll self-deport

You're famous with low lives so you think this is it but it's a ceiling you've hit/can't go beyond it.

Works like a top: accused of racism, we pay up.

Herd works off mutual energy like a flock of birds assuming the flight pattern is correct, surely.

Labeled our customs, culture/traditions as bigoted, intolerant, repressive and discriminatory.

If left approves cuz you reinforce their weirdness they'll love you but you're going to hell miss.

Cashmere allergy: There's just too many fibers, the reason for comfort yet chemical misery.

I get sick right away with cashmere, too much opportunity for toxic chemicals holding onto her.

Don't wear used clothes. Previous detergents/where they've been/who they are...think of it dear.

 **Send them back or they'll keep coming**

A free society requires high IQ populations, and there is not one low IQ pop on earth that is free.

They obscure the doctrine of judgement cuz they don't want their sins judged, they love em.

Justin Trudeau has never uttered a syllable that was not a gross platitude of stupidity. Gareth Rydal

Ever noticed how the most popular are twits?

They hate Trump cuz hating white people is the trend but especially a patriarch worth billions.

They get power over you thru intimidation, so if you have no fear (like Trump) how can they win?

One can never know when he will be done until that moment he's done. Thank you Albert Einstein

News never tells truth cuz they don't know it, don't want you to know it or been told not to say it.

Grandstanding: Making videos about a tragic event and making it all about you instead.

Grandstand: Using your personal tragedy to become famous and rich (spot light on the bitch).

If you don't like it don't come here that's how it works.

Political Islam is parallel societies and radical tendencies.

The Jezebel spirit puts down your husband like it's a feminist thing: It's in most women, fear it.

He calls his wife "Mama" and she treats him like a baby. Is this pathetic, what do you think?

After forgiveness everything falls into place. You don't elect or plan are just carried away.

I didn't say I believed her I just told you what she said but you gotta see this messenger's pathetic.

Traumatized lose boundaries then the problem floods in creating insanity. Lesson: stay calm always.

We lost our defenses when told "they're all good" and to be welcoming to the depraved dunces.

Guests: they burrow in then can't get rid of em. Like fish after 3 days they smell, just sayin'.

Thrift store gems: the point is I can't know who wore them before me.

It's not so much women vote thru emotion but phony virtue signaling for temporary thrill of ego.

They wanna put the whole blame on the men who are mild and rational compared to women.

If you criticize her behavior it means you don't like her: refusing correction marks the immature.

They think they can have things both ways--it's doublethink saying it's ok to be contradictory.

You gotta make your marriage work for in these latter days the default setting is becoming jerks.

Many men marry a body and when it changes it's over but a spiritual connection endures all weather.

They have no respect for what marriage is all about.

She couldn't resist what she did cuz she is what she is—the wicked never question what they want to do, sis.

70% of blended families fail ending in divorce. Having been a (failed) stepmother I know this.

Men are weak cuz their dads were gone, brought up by mom--its her anger when they speak.

Would you wanna be married to you? Yet your spouse is required to suffer whether male or female.

You don't know what trouble is 'til you get into a blended family where there's no peace only dis.

A blended family won't work like a first-marriage one: identity struggles and jealousy triangles.

Culture is now anti-marriage even as they redefine it. Divorce is "in"--her fem friends encourage it.

With all these interlocking jealousy patterns one's health degrades and the nerves frazzled.

Tho' happy in simplicity a blended family is complex identity struggles, anger, balancing forces.

Satan's minions are often very good lookin' cuz Lucifer's handsome so always think opposite.

No matter what God can heal your marriage.

Women always hugging/screaming since they saw the housewives did it-- please don't hug me.

Unquestioning, unconditional and pathetic maternalism of Merkel to foreigners/leech interlopers.

Without correct view their speech is so boring, hitting on the wrong points, showcasing.

In fact everything's that way, the incorrect view creates a mess and so goes also your enemy.

Studies show women are more violent than men but we don't hear much domestic violence against them.

Why is mom so angry? Because she's a feminist not a sweet little lady like those from the fifties.

Housekeeper make it shine/smell good not just push the dust around/not quite clean no-good.

Trudeau: male feminist caught in a grope. Watch the drama teacher get outa this one, the dope.

But the new maid does not-quite-clean, no sheen. House should smell nice and have a shine.

Part of the Jezebel Spirit is to disappear for awhile, to fear it, to wonder what you did to deserve it?

Holy Household. No more leaky boat syndrome (gossip, outgroup preferences) but home/gold.

Blacks are angry because they don't have a father in the home and reflect a bitter mother.

Since men don't like macho women, what's gonna happen?

I'd never ever leave you honey cuz I know you'd be lost without me.

That's the thing, you don't divorce husband cuz they suicide or become hopelessly lost, boss.

Most women below fifty are immoral and it's proven by what they vote for like abortion and more.

My Ph.D. in Streets: Small desert town filled with feminists, living in cabin way out to get away from em.

Just so she can be a social justice warrior for a day + 15 minutes fame she causes trouble, ok?

The biggest myths meaning death of a country: masculinity is toxic and down on patriarchy. START

Maybe that's her destiny, maybe it isn't, either way it is none of my business.

Grandstanding: turning the event into her stage or opportunity to virtue signal like a sage.

Alcoholism is where you're drinking more and earlier. "Post time" keeps moving up until it's breakfast with beer.

Self-forgive for all you did when used by demons sis (like when you henpecked husband/DISSED).

100 KAREN KELLOCK BOOKS

AFFINITY OR MISERY
AGELESS CORNUCOPIA
AMERICA AWAKE!
AMERICA'S DAFT ERA
ARTS OF PALEO FASTING
AUTOPHAGY ON CHEATERS
BACKSTABBING NEUROTICS
BETRAYAL TRAUMA
BOOMERS AND BROKENNESS
BOOT ON NECK
CHAMPION GUIDES
COMMIE NUTHOUSE
COMMIES
COMMUNIST SPIRIT
CONTAGION OF MADNESS
CONTAGIOUS MADNESS
CULTURE CLASH BASHED
DAFT LEFT
DAILY FASTARIAN
DAM RATS
DIVERSITY IS CRUELTY
E-RACE WHITE
EVIL FREAKS (Beyond Gross)
THE END OR A BEND?
FEMALE BULLIES AND FEMI-NAZIS
FEMALE CARNALITY
FEMALE DUMB DOWN
FEMALE POWER DRIVE
FEMINISM AND RUIN 1 & 2
FIX FOR MISFITS
FOOLS & TRAMPS
FREEDOM SPEAKING
FRENEMY ENABLER
FRENEMY LIAR
FRENEMY THIEF
FRENEMY TRAITOR
TRENEMY TYRANT
GENIUS IS HELD DOWN
GLOBALISLAM
GOD USES THE FLAWED
HAZE OF THE LATTER DAYS

AUTHOR BIO
Karen Kellock Ph.D.

Ph.D Political Psychology, UCI 1976
Post-Doctoral: UCI Medical School
Department of Psychiatry
Grants NIMH, NIAAA

Ph.D. dissertation "A Systems-Theoretic View of Pathologic Interaction" made an early mark as the "Wife of the Alcoholic Syndrome". Postdoctoral research at UCI Medical, Dept. of Psychiatry on the systems surrounding pathology on NIMH and NIAAA federal grants: The Contagion of Madness: The Psychology of Neurotic Interaction and Pathological Systems. Therapy tool Therapeutic Playwriting introduced the play Mary and Murv: Gruesome Twosomes in the Alcoholic Marriage. She taught Abnormal Psychology and Pathological Systems Theory at UC and CSU campuses and developed "the Debris Theory of Disease" in 100 books and website: (www.karenkellock.org).